Set Me Free

Unapologetically Me

By

J Mi'chelle

Copyright © 2025 J Mi'chelle

All rights reserved.

No part of this publication may be reproduced, stored in a retrieval system, or transmitted in any form or by any means electronic, mechanical, photocopying, recording, or otherwise without the prior written permission of the author, except in the case of brief quotations embodied in critical articles or reviews.

DEDICATIONS

I dedicate this book of poems to everyone who has inspired me.

Jamey Brown Jr - The writer of the family. You have always inspired me. As a child, I wanted to be just like you and write books. I felt as if I was not detailed enough to write, but then I realized that my poems were enough. Thank you for always being the great writer you are and showing me that believing in myself is possible.

Akeya' Harris - Thank you for believing in my poems from the beginning. Since middle school, you have always read my poems and told me that they create vivid pictures where my words come to life. Because of that, I had faith that I could truly create something great.

Winifred Arthur & Brianna Akers - Thank you for inspiring me. It was with you all that I began creating poems.

Empress Bey - Thank you for allowing me to be open with you, for giving me ideas, and for helping me create a safe space to write freely.

Jamal Washington - Thank you for pushing me and pouring life into me when I needed it the most. Thank you for showing me that I truly have a gift.

Shakyvia Sanders, Marina Maye, Leonard Roberson & Shakhiska Wilkins – Thank you for all the love and support you've shown throughout my journey of writing this book.

A NOTE TO MY READERS:

Thank you for choosing to embrace this journey with me! This book of poetry is about all the emotions I have experienced and the desires of my heart. I hope that this book of poetry helps inspire you to be your best self and to know that we all can relate to one another. Allow this poetry to flow through you and help you embrace every experience you have been through in this thing we call life. Embrace the journey, and appreciate the good and the bad!

TABLE OF CONTENTS

Chapter 1: The Romance of Love 1

    Deeper Than the Surface 2
    You are the One 3
    What You Mean to Me 5
    Love 6
    Know You Better 8
    Playlist 9
    The Dance of Romance 10
    With You 11
    Play a Tune for Me (Sonnet Number 2) 12
    Dreams 13
    The Sentiment of You 14
    Temporary Feels 16
    Beautiful Eyes 17
    Funny 18
    Love Without Fear 20
    Set Me Free: When Love First Speaks 22

Chapter 2: Deep Waters – Falling & Floating 23

    The True Meaning of it All 24
    Fact or Fiction 25
    Two Lonely Hearts 26
    A Bleeding Heart 27
    Our Love 28
    Clear Skies 30
    Fading Fireworks 32
    Disillusioned 33
    Cake 34
    DMs & Likes 35
    Little Water Bottle Girl 36
    Pieces of the Heart 38
    Wolves in Sheep's Clothing 39

Black Heron 41
Set Me Free: Living in the In-Between 42

Chapter 3: The Breaking Point 43

Farewell 44
A Thief in the Night 46
Broken Promises 48
Who Are You? 50
Caged 52
The Cost of Being Right 53
The Day the Earth Stood Still 54
Generational Curses 56
Chaos 57
Your Smile 58
Set Me Free: When It Hurts 60

Chapter 4: To Heal all Areas 61

I Choose Me 62
Blank Canvas 63
Moments 64
Walking with Purpose 65
Surrender 66
Know Thy Self 67
The Force Awakens 68
Still Swimming 69
Healing Her 70
Vision 71
Little Birdie 72
Set Me Free: Echoes & Endings – Letting Go 73

Chapter 5: Where Confidence Begins 74

Beauty 75
Good Girl 76
Noir 77
Shy Butterfly 78
Out of Order 79

Juelz 80
Brown Sugar Queen 81
She is Worth Loving 82
My Girlfriends 83
Hush Controversy 85
The Makings of Me 87
I Know That I Am Greatness 88
Set Me Free: Soft Landings & New Beginnings 90

Soundtracks to the Poetry 91

Letter to myself

I write from the heart
From the parts that I don't like to show
However, I am here to let those parts glow

I will no longer let those parts slumber
I have awaken something so deep
I know it will set me free

To be able to breathe again
And release anything that was holding me back
To see the world in a different light
And appreciate this journey called life

No longer will I let the pain swallow me whole
I chose to be bold
And to let go
Set me free

Chapter 1:
The Romance of Love

Deeper Than the Surface

I want to know what lies beneath
I know it is more to you
Show me what makes you tick
Could you really be open with me?

Could you show me all the wonders of your heart?
Even the parts that only shows in the dark
Could we ever be deeper than the surface?
I hope I am not making you nervous

I just want to see what makes you, you
Like what things make you blue
I want to see the inner beauty of you
I would love to share intimate moments with you

Could we be in that moment?
Where no one else matters but us
Where we are sharing a time in space
That no one can erase

I want to know a deeper side of you
I want to learn you
From the inner workings of you to the workings of your body
Like what makes you naughty
Like what turns you on
And even what turns you off

I want to know you on all intimate levels
Let me get to know you... Mentally, emotionally, spiritually,
and last one not least sexually

You are the One

When my mind goes blank
You the only person I see
When my mind goes blank
You be the one that I need
When my mind goes blank
My heart just bleeds
When my mind goes blank
I just believe
When my mind goes blank
You the only one that I need

Kissing you, missing you
My love always stay true
You're forever my boo
Just me n you

Homies like no other
You will never find another
Powerful is what we are
Together we can reach the stars
And nothing can tear us apart

U caught my attention by your humor
Laughter filled the room
Me n you were such in-tune
Your eyes met mines
N love filled the room
From that day our love bloom

Your love has taken me to a place where I have never been

When my mind goes blank
You the only person I see
When my mind goes blank
You be the one that I need
When my mind goes blank
My heart just bleeds
When my mind goes blank
I just believe
When my mind goes blank
You the only that one I need

What You Mean to Me

Never in a million years, would I thought you would become
my favorite person
Someone I wanted to spend all my time with
It's the way you make me smile that's brings warmth to my
heart
There is never a dull moment with you
We truly enjoyed each other's company
Even when you make me the angriest
I cannot stay mad at you
I just love talking to you
You truly lift my spirits up
You hate to see me sad, so you always tried to cheer me up
Moments where it is just us are the best
You love to play fight, and I will end it by just laying on your
chest
To see you in your element keeps me intrigued
Your energy is filled with love, laughter, and positivity
You are a vibe
Even when you are down, I want to support you in every way
If people saw you the way, I see you
They would know that you were something to treasure each
and everyday

Love

The True Essence of Love

A love that will continue to grow even if time stood still
A love that's never forced at will
A love that's true blue
A pure love between me and you

The True Essence of Love

A love that doesn't manipulate
A love that's graceful
A love that's unconditional
A love that's personal

The True Essence of Love

A love that is gentle and innocent
A love that is so genuine, that it fills your spirit
A love that makes you believe that anything is possible
A love that's never ends even when one passes
A love that makes you proud
A love where two people become one

The True Essence of Love

A love that shares intimacy
A love that leaves a legacy
A love that gets better with time
A love that's hard to find
A love that creates a union

A love that seeps through your vein
A love that will always remain

The True Essence of Love

Know You Better

I would like to get to know you better
I think I am the type of girl you could be down for
You give off the vibes
That makes me want to know more

I want to know more about you
Right now, I am on the outside looking in
Somehow, you are grabbing my attention
And I don't want to lose focus

Maybe it's your smile that leaves me mesmerized
The laid-back vibe, that makes me want to spend all night and day with you
The taste you have in music that makes me want to have conversations with you
The parent figure in you, that makes me see the greatness in you

Mmhmm, maybe I am crushing
Yea, you got me blushing
But I got to play it cool
I know in due time, you'll be coming around soon

Playlist

If I could create the perfect playlist, it will be all about you
A blend of sweet and soft melodies, that connects to the soul
Instrumentals full of passion and love
Songs that really make you want to fall in love

I would describe every part of you through rhythm and blues
You are my sweetest taboo
You are the rain against my windowpane
And I love the way you make me rain

Let me serenade you, deep into the night
Let me tell you how I feel over an 808 beat
Let me give you the best of me

Could I be this woman's worth that Maxwell was talking about?
Let us see what "could it be"
Like the Tevin Campbell song…
Put on the Mary Jane Girls, we could go all night long

The Dance of Romance

How would you feel if I told you I miss you?
What if I told you I want to kiss you?
And feel your sweet embrace
You are really making my heart race

I miss you whispering sweet things in my ear
And bringing my body near
You holding me in your arms
Kissing me on my forehead
Then you turn me around
And we begin to slow dance

Moving to the beautiful melodies
I know this love will have longevity
You make me think of marital bliss
Just from kissing your lips

Can we have just one more dance?
So we can get back to the romance

With You

The water is still
The sun is fading
The atmosphere around the horizon is filled with orange and pink
The stars are starting to fill the sky

The smell of summer is in the air
There is a slight breeze, and I can feel it on my skin
The sound of the porch swing is in the distance
There's beautiful laugher everywhere

You are standing beside me
I curl up in your arms
And we drift into the scenery
We are in this moment with the outside world
However, all I see is you

This is how I know
That no matter where life takes me
I will always have everything, I need with you beside me

Play a Tune for Me (Sonnet Number 2)

Shall I compare thee to a beautiful tune?
The beat of your heart plays a melody for me
Sweet and serene like a spring's day afternoon
The sounding beats of your heart has harmony
The closer I am, the faster it beats
I can imagine your voice in a falsetto form
The feelings of passion is making me weak
The chorus of your heart is keeping me warm
I can feel the flutters of your heart
It sings a beautiful hook
It is a striking scenery of art
I can tell that you do not want to be apart

Let us play our notes in unison
We can go places that we have never been

Dreams

Last night, I dreamt of you in color
Flashes of you imprinted in my brain
Could you be everything I desire?
Someone I could admire?
I only see you when I am asleep...
Involuntary thoughts of you during REM sleep
These vivid dreams seem so realistic
These dreams are so simplistic
Simple pleasures of laughing with you, holding hands, and becoming friends
It's something that just feels nostalgic
So please do not wake me
I would love to see how this dream ends...

The Sentiment of You

She sets the mood
Candlelight by the bamboo
She puts on her favorite mix
While she lights the piff

She is softly curated
I think to myself, she can't be duplicated
I am admiring from the other side of the room
Her skin is as plush as the clouds in the sky
Listening to her speak is a sweet lullaby

We are sharing the same thoughts
But we begin the romance
In intellectual dialogue
We both giving the same head nod

It's a once-in-a-lifetime experience
I ain't never felt like this
It is intriguing
She got me feeling like a brand new being

Stimulations of the brain
It is sending electrical currents through my body
Could she be my shorty?
My one and only

Only time will tell
I want to flow with her
Peeling back the layers that lies beneath
I think she is so unique

Your vibrations sending me into shock
The jolt awakes me as I await our next encounter
Currents moving loud, but I hope this message is even louder

Temporary Feels

His love was like an interlude
After the first taste, I wanted more
I wanted to explore
To really see what he had in store

He left me breathless
The feeling was temporary
But it was imprinted into my brain for a lifetime
To feel this way should be a crime

He had me jones'in down to my bones
It's a feeling I never wanted to leave alone
All I could hear was the interlude he had my body playing
He truly had my body raining

Satisfactions of sweet-fullness
We're down to our last kiss
Let this moment be treasured
By the interlude fading out to the mesmerizing sounds of pleasure

Beautiful Eyes

Today is bright and sunny
As the breeze passes by, he caught my eye
He's starring in my direction, and we locked eyes
I didn't want to look away

Never have I seen something so serene
His eyes were beautiful
I was locked in his gaze
His eyes were seductive and charming
Once he has your attention, his eyes read your soul
He's looking at me naked
He sees all of me
My fears, my joy, my wants, and my needs
It's making me weak

I continue to stare and smile back
The feelings are mutual
I don't want to go into overdrive
I gotta put this thing in neutral

What a beautiful man
I think I'm his biggest fan
I want to explore every part of him
From head to toe, front limb to limb

I think I met my match
But it's too soon to get attached
I gotta take it easy
I want this to last
I don't want this just to be something in my past

Funny

He stands in front of me and I see a reflection of myself
It's as if he's mirroring me through his eyes
I don't know if I am ready
The manifestation of it all is too real
This man is definitely the real deal

I've been yearning for something true
The ultimate love between two humans
I pray for patience
I don't want to mess this up
I want to pray with this man, that's how I know what I want is genuine

I thought intent and purposeful was the way to be
Maybe my emotions are getting the best of me

You say you will, but you don't
You want to be the captain of this boat
So I say lets float
The troubling water of pressure is pushing you away
So maybe we're not on the same page

My feelings are deeper than the abyss
But that's just who I am
Don't be like the others and toy with me
Please believe that I am everything

But if you can't see that, be man enough to speak your truth
I'm living proof…

I'm living proof of a woman that nurtures from inside and out
A woman that loves wholeheartedly
A woman that knows true beauty lies in both the light and dark

I am not superficial
I am something real
I am in touch with what makes me feel
I am more than worldly
My faith is attached to my emotions
My devotion is to love and be loved
By first God and myself

If you see me truly with those lovely eyes
You'll see the beauty of what makes me, me

So wake up!
Stop sleeping on me
and see the spiritual being

Love Without Fear

I am as free
as a bird who flaps her wings in the wild.
Love should unfold
freely—without restrictions,
without jurisdictions.
I don't stand in the way of love.

To relish in a love
that's open and kind,
so clear even the blind could see.
I see you—
and I was willing to face any pressures
just to give us the chance
to explore something
that could make all our experiences worthwhile.

Always remember—
connections can bring blessings.
God wouldn't place a carrot in front of you
and then say, *you can't have it*.
You just have to be willing
to open your mind,
and understand the value
of love's being—
when it's genuine,
when it's something you can't resist.

But if it's not…
then this moment wasn't meant to be free.

Because love asks us
to see beyond the limitations of our mind.

And the beauty of it all is—
we are neither bitter nor broken.
We understand now:
love requires more than desire.
It requires courage,
and truth.

So I'll carry you
like a memory that almost bloomed.
But our friendship will never be doomed.

We lived in our moment—
and it was sweet,
because of our honesty.
You'll always be dear to me.

Set Me Free: Unapologetically Me

The Playlist

When Love First Speaks

1. Love – Art of Noise
2. The Sweetest Taboo – Sade
3. Cheers 2 U – Playa
4. Angel – Smooth Jazz All Stars
5. A Long Walk – Jill Scott
6. It Never Rains (In Southern California) – Tony! Toni! Toné!

Chapter 2:
Deep Waters – Falling & Floating

The True Meaning of it All

I felt the most comfortable with you
You handle me as if I was something that you would never want to break
As if, I was fragile
You saw the beauty in me even when I could not see it myself
When your eyes glazed upon my eyes
It was as if you could see my soul
You spoke to the essence of my soul
You made me believe in love
Being with you was like no other
Somehow, we still ended in turmoil
It was as if we could not get this love thing right
Nevertheless, we loved each other so deeply
You saw me for me, and that's all I ever asked for in a lover
True soul mates indeed
Even though we are not together and will never be again
I would relive every moment I spent with you
I felt protected in your arms
You always made me feel alive
And every day, you gave me butterflies
When I think of love, your face is what I see
What I felt for you was so real
Crazy part is I will never get that love from you again
I cherished what we had
But I believe one day I'll find it again
And when I do this time, it will be for life
Something that will never end
A love that I can create my own happiness and family with
I thank you for showing me that love is real
I thank you for showing me love is obtainable
And with that I know that my love is something special

Fact or Fiction

How can I shake this feeling?
How can you tell me what we shared was not real
As if, it meant nothing to you
It is deeper than just sex
Or maybe you never looked beyond that
I showed you the inner workings of me
I became vulnerable with you and l let my guard down
I thought I was able to be free around you
We floated in a way that kept us in sync
There was a point where we were inseparable
To me, we were magical
But I was living in a fantasy thinking we could ever be more
You fed me lies as if you was someone I could count on
As if, you were dependable
But in the end, you were selfish to a degree that was so
complex, you wanted me to believe I was delusional
How could you ever say we wasn't intimate
Do you even understand the definition of intimacy?
We were beyond the level of friendship
But you too immature to feel that

Two Lonely Hearts

Separated by pain and misery
I know you are missing me
There is no change
Now all we have is heartache and pain

You departed from me because the loving got hard
Now we are two lonely hearts
You say you want me back
But at what cost?

I do not want to be misunderstood
Why can't you see that the love was good?
I wanted us to grow and learn together
I know this is a storm we can weather

Walking side by side, we can stride
Past all the fears we used to hide
For what we have built could never be fake
I know this is not a mistake

A Bleeding Heart

Out running the past seems to never last
Somehow, I'm still trapped in the sinking hole
Waves of grief within a sea of scars
But I choose to still fight, I'm seeing the light
I'm climbing mountains
You reach for me, seeing inside my soul
I finally decided to take the support
Hanging on a cliff, I hope you don't let go
Your fingers start to slip
It's too much for you to handle
I'm losing my grip
You reach out again
But there was no effort
And now I'm falling

Our Love

With each heartbreak there is a stage of acceptance
Accepting that this really happen and I have to move on
I try my best to learn from the situation to understand how to love better
I try to learn what it is that I am truly searching for in a lover
I ask myself what is the ideal person for me

This heartbreak was truly different from any other
To love someone and not have that same love in return will question everything you know about yourself
I told myself I will never fall for someone if the feelings aren't mutual
And with you, I always felt that they were
It was a feeling that resonated with us

Reminiscing about the times, we shared
I am thinking about the bond we created
And how you was always my favorite
It was moments that we shared that made me believe that the love was real

The love that I felt was deeper than just friendship or even romantic
I begin to see you as family
I seen you as someone that I never want to lose
I felt that you was not only here for a season but for a lifetime

I can truly say that my love for you was unconditional
No matter if you was right or wrong, I never loved you any

less
I never judged you

I felt that you love me the same way....
Unconditionally
Until I realized you was losing love for me and treating me differently
There was a change and with that change your love turn into conditional love

I like to think that we both loved each other unconditionally
But with our unconditional love, we loved differently
With the actions on how we loved, we begin to not be compatible
Our loving styles were not suitable for one another
And in the end, we lost the most important thing
US

Clear Skies

What's the value of friendship now a days?
All these silly games we play
Toyed with my heart and now I can't look at you the same

There's nothing left and I'm feeling empty
I seen you switch up on me in an instance
Now we both seem distance

Consequences we have to face
A detachment, in fact
Somehow, we got off track

No more lies, no more games
This shit is really lame
N now we placing blame

What's holding you back?
Courage and truth is what you lack

Wasted time, wasted energy, wasted space
I have to bow out with grace

I put myself in situations that I thought I could face
But in the end, I played myself, to ever think you could be the man for me
How could I ever believe?
That you would be down for me

I seen the signs and knew the truth since the beginning
Man… who was I kidding?

To put my trust in you and tell you my truth

I chose a path where I knew the road would end
A road of destruction
Something that I knew wouldn't function

I played myself all the way to the left
And now you won't even talk to me
There's no respect
And that's something, I won't leave uncheck

Fading Fireworks

I can hear the sounds of deep explosions
There are crackles, booms and even whistles
As my heart flutters
I'm in a daze
The night skies are beautiful
There's laughter all around
What a joyful occasion
But eventually it comes to an end
Nothing lasts forever
Fireworks are seen as seasonal
But what a beauty it could be to see them every night
But one must think, because boredom can strike
Or do we just lose interest
Looking for sparks
Now we're lost in the translation of it all
The fireworks are fading
And now you're just a vivid memory that will turn into dust
eventually

Disillusioned

Fall was my first love
Fiery and wild
The passion was so sweet
Loving to our own beat
But the leaves started to fall

Winter approached
Smooth and cool while snowflakes fell over the Horizon
You bundled me up in your arms
It felt good when you loved me from behind
But we slowly became distance and selfishness filled the room

Spring arose to the occasion
Like my knight in shining armor
You were such a charmer
Smile was beautiful as black sand
I explored things with you that I never had before
But it was all an illusion
I met the representation of you

Summer came with excitement
The connection made me believe we could conquer anything
This season was different
I just melted every time I was by you
I couldn't let this season pass me by
I held on tight until it burnt me up on the inside like the earth's core

What a world wind of emotions
These seasons were so captivating
But it costed me my heart

Cake

The slice of the cake is soft and warm
It's a sweetness that melts in your mouth
But the piece doesn't last for long
Here within this moment I'm wanting more
But once I have eaten it, it's all gone
I keep telling myself you can't have it both ways
Do I save it or eat it?

They say you can't hold joy and never lose.
You can't pick paths and skip the dues.
You can't love deep and not get bruised
You can't eat cake and keep it, too.

As I relive the moment of the sweetest escape
I remember how he fell in love with just the friendship
He draws to my beauty like he's hypnotized
And now I have him wrapped around my finger
I have him right where I want him

I want more
More loving
More excitement
More fun

But I want another type of cake
And now I'm back to reality
He's staring at me from the other side of the room
I'm feeling a cinematic boom
Who said you can't have your cake and eat it too?

DMs & Likes

Who wants to play make believe?
Social media is a fairytale land
A world full of lies & deceit
Boy, don't play with me

A few thousand likes & some DMs
Oh, don't let that go to your head
He wants me & he wants me
And he wants me too
I mean, it could all be true

Now we choosing
Could it be, they're all the wrong picks
You fell in love with the thought of me and my body
What about my mind?
Oh, you must think I'm blind?

To not think that I can't see through you
You're transparent as a glass windowpane
Ima need for you to stay in your lane
Because you'll never get the chance to speak to me again

You thought you was going to get me in bed
Now you left on read
You're mental is very malnourished
Hopefully one day you can flourish

Little Water Bottle Girl

Things happened that I just can't explain
But I know this one brought me pain
I had to laugh to stop the tears
I'm asking myself, how did I get here?

I told myself, let's try something new
Man, that shit had me so confused
He's really into me
And all I want to do is leave

This Little Water Bottle Girl is trippin'
I'm trippin' over my feelings & his
He treated me so well
Something that every woman should experience
But my heart wasn't in it

We took it to the next level
It left me speechless
This wasn't what I needed
Little Water Bottle Girl just go home

You're not happy here
This is something you can't force
He can even hear it in your voice

Little Water Bottle Girl's well never runs dry
But she didn't explode to the magnitude that she's use to
His touch didn't make her melt
There was no connection

Now I'm sitting here feeling empty
I have to fill my bottle back up
What you are searching for is in the near future
But right now, Little Water Bottle Girl
You must choose yourself

Pieces of the Heart

Matters of a lonely heart
I can feel my soul turning dark
Yearning for a connection
In a world that's so unpleasant

My Heart is turning cold
It's the same story that's always told
Feeling lost

You were never mine
Trying to keep you, was like holding water in my hands
You slipped through the cracks of me

Every tear felt like a thousand cuts
I had to rid myself of you
I released all feelings of you until my heart was drained
I released the pain
Told myself I'll never give my all again

Wolves in Sheep's Clothing

Uncertain feelings creeped up upon me like a slow chill upon my spine
I couldn't shake the feelings that something wasn't right
I knew I had to distance myself because I didn't want to put up a fight
The feeling felt too familiar

But this time, something was different.
It felt forced, and I could never tell if it was genuine

I was hurt in many different ways
But I remain honest and stood firm on what I believed
I didn't have the capacity to deal with this again
My feelings weren't the same either

Either way, I knew it wasn't a line that I would ever cross
Feelings weren't mutual
I thought this time it could be platonic
But it wasn't working
To me, it was wolves in sheep's clothing

How could I continue something that was so taboo?
All I wanted was a true friendship
To know my pain, my struggle, and most of all what I truly loved
How could one still want, what I wasn't offering

Friendship and trust are something that is earned but also one must be deserving
Friendship and trust shouldn't be given so easily

We grew closer and closer
But it seem as if they wanted more
I couldn't offer them what they were seeking

Most don't understand with titles come expectations
I never want to put a serious title on things because I knew I
didn't want those expectations
I was unavailable and made myself clear
We continue the friendship

As time progressed conversation always change to curiosity
There were mysteries that I didn't want to unlock
He painted himself as someone that could treat me better
than any other friend
But in the end, he was just the same

Black Heron

Seeing through your tactics in the daylight
Foolish to think, one is so gullible
A false sense of trust that you created as if you were friendly

Black Heron

Respect is earned and not given
Genuineness is driven by the power of love, morals, and standards
It's integrity that connects to the characteristics of a person
It's the warmth that one feels by being in one's presence

That is something you lack
Black Heron, How could you ever treat someone so unjust?
It's small minded in fact

I come from a place of empathy and wholeness
A place to empower, not to devour
A place of love and kindness
But please don't be fooled
You cross that line, and the soul reaper will be coming for you

Set Me Free: Unapologetically Me

The Playlist

Living in the In-Between

7. Living Inside Your Love – Earl Klugh
8. After the Dance (Vocal) – Marvin Gaye
9. The Sweetest Thing – Lauryn Hill
10. Everything – Mary J. Blige
11. Latch (feat. Sam Smith) – Disclosure
12. Pretty Wings (Uncut) – Maxwell

Chapter 3: The Breaking Point

Farewell

Farewell to the memories that we once shared
I gotta lay my feelings bare
I let the current flow
I let them wash away and say my goodbyes

I have accepted the change
Letting autumn take the leaves and planting roots in the shifting soil

This isn't a sad song
It feels good to finally release
To move on and accept that we can't find happiness in each other

Wishing the best for us both
This was a lesson learned that I needed
It's going to make me better

I give myself grace
The next chapter in my life
I will take my time

I won't be cold, but I will be guarded
And recognize what's real
So I'll cry happy tears
Because I'll get a chance to find real love
A key that fits without force

Let the right one come to me with a warm embrace
A sweet taste fill with honesty, trust, understanding and love
Here's my farewell to you
I leave that feeling of heartache with the universe and let it combust

A Thief in the Night

He comes to steal your heart,
Lurking in the shadows of the dark.
This won't be an easy mark.
To take what's scarce,
He creates the ultimate disguise—
Something so smooth, it's considered art.

As he admires her beauty,
He thinks of what-ifs—
The idea of having her to himself.
He knows she's off-limits,
But he wants control.

He moves swiftly in the night
And steals her joy—
Sly as a fox,
Trusted like a man's best friend.
But this dog bites.

Letting her think that their kiss means forever—
He stays just long enough to feel clever.
He wants her soft. He wants her sweet.
But a woman like that don't live in deceit.

So he continues his disguise
Of being the nice guy.
He makes her believe—
He's nothing like the guys in her past.
This time it's gonna last.

As he watches his prey,
He hopes that she'll be all his one day…

**But what you stole, you couldn't keep—
Because hearts don't live in hands that creep.**

Broken Promises

Promises I made to myself I never keep
Mix emotions are making me weep
It's something in me that I can't explain
Turmoil is causing so much pain
I think my pride is getting in my way

I say I won't, but I do what I please
But these decisions I make, I can't keep my mind at ease
I toy with the emotion of joy
It's like I'm losing sleep from all the noise
The noise in my mind
I can't keep them quiet
And I'm starting to hurt by it
I know the right thing to do but it doesn't correlate with my wants
I keep telling myself focus on the needs
But my heart bleeds
I'm yearning for a love
But am I ready?

Promises to cherish myself and love on me
That's all I really need
Empowering myself to believe I can be happy
Not to settle for meaningless conversations and passions that don't last
Things that's covered under a mask
I gotta let go of the past
Let go of the hurt & pain
What I'm doing right now is a terrible game
I'm toying with my own heart

I can't fall apart
So I'm starting this journey to become whole again
This time I'm going to win
Win the battle within
And in due time, I will heal
And be able to feel the true meaning of love & happiness

Who Are You?

Tainted Soul

I don't want to be defined by my adversary
I know what I have been through helps to make the person I am today
But I am more than the hurt & pain
Sometimes I feel that there's a black cloud over me that I can't escape
The hurt & pain comes from every direction
And here I am with my back against the wall trying to face them all

But with everything I'm going through, I still stand tall
I think what hurts the most is when you let someone in and they see all the imperfections of you, and all they see is a tainted soul

With all that lies inside of me
There is still beauty
There is grace
There is meaning
There is love
There is Joy
This is someone who is worth loving

All I ever wanted was the simple things in life
To be loved, to have love, to create my own destiny, to create family, and enjoy all the simple moments in life

It's the simple things that brings the most joy
From a smile to even a simple moment like hearing the leaves
blow in the breeze

All we have is love, and that's all we need

Sometimes love is the hardest thing to reach

Still, I reach for love — flowing through meaning, carried by
understanding

Caged

The bars are closing in
I'm unable to reach the open door
Drowned by hurt and sorrow
I can't recognize what's real

Holding on to people and memories that I should of been let go of
Giving everything a fighting chance
But what am I holding on too
Being too forgiving is a double edge sword

I can see the path that I need to take
But I'm afraid of what awaits
I am embarking on a new journey
I have to embrace change
If what I been going through has been the worst yet
Then why am I scared of a new path?
Love and loyalty shouldn't be this hard
Love shouldn't cause this much pain

I can see the open door
The caged of not letting go is unsettling
But I have the power to unlock the cage and be set free
I work through the fear and see what's awaiting me
Holding on to my faith, my morals, my truth, and the lessons learned
There's nothing to fear
I have to let go in order to not be cage anymore

The Cost of Being Right

Writings on the wall can be unwritten
Opinions are oversaturated with judgment
Humans' definition of righteousness is based upon one's own experience
Emotion and logic is getting the best of us

Who am I to tell you what's right and what's wrong
Just because you have an opinion doesn't mean you should weigh in
There's room for growth and understanding
They say the truth matter… but what about kindness?
What about timing?
The connections that one holds can be fragile

Accountability, can cost friendships
The writings on the wall can lead to misinterpretation
Everyone comprehends things differently and
It can be the cost of relationships

It carries emotional weight and moral tension
The questions of love and loyalty blur the lines –
And reason unravels
Comprehension between friends seem so far in the distance
You ask yourself, how did we get here
I let go of my convictions and realized…
That my integrity to myself means much, much more

The Day the Earth Stood Still

Only seventeen, with a bright future
I knew that I was on the journey of becoming a young adult,
making a mark in this world
Knowing that I was destined for greatness
But I was still innocent

September 4th, 2009 changed everything for me
No longer innocent
The weight of the world, my world, fell on my shoulders
I understood death, but it truly never affected me until that
day

I lost something that I could never get back
It was stolen from me
I felt abandoned
I felt alone
I felt lost
And most of all, my joy was gone

Sleepless nights and days
Where was I mentally
I felt detached from my own body
I was just a walking zombie

Never truly cared about nothing after that day
My favorite line became if I die, I die
How could I survive without you?
How could I go on?

With pain like that
What else is there to say?
We've experienced so much pain in our family
And that day was the icing on the cake

Generational Curses

The pain flows into a cycle that feels never ending
It's hard to even find the beginning
A never ending loop of dismay

There's no more color, no brightness
I'm surrounded around darkness
How do I break free?
From all the negativity

It's imprinted on my past
I recognize the patterns
I see what it's doing to my family
I tell myself no more

I feel the weight of the world on my shoulder
It's caving in on me
I must be set free
Release me from the shackles

I will break every chain
The change starts with me
I'm getting sick from the motions
I no longer want to live in dysfunction

I choose to heal
I choose to forgive
I choose to understand
I choose boundaries
I chose love
(But most importantly I choose me)

Chaos

Born in a world of chaos
How could I know what peace is like
Peace is enjoying intimate moments
Having precious memories with love ones
What my peace is may be different from yours
Just know through chaos you still can find Joy

Your Smile

Your smile was vivid in color
Illuminating the whole room without even trying
Your energy was so powerful—
And it all started with your smile

Wishing to create new moments with you
To hear your voice again
To feel your laughter touch my soul
Your laughter – so beautiful and bold

I tell myself to never take things for granted
My soul was shook
But I leaned on faith
Because I believe you're in a better place

I hold onto all the good memories
Even the bad
I remember all the life lessons you gave me
Wiser than your years on this earth
You're still teaching us in your spiritual form
You were really before your time

I truly cherished our relationship
Too many can't say they had the love we had
Our sibling bond was so true
It's something that could never be tethered

You motivated us to be great
From you being more than a big brother
To us, you were our 2nd father

Protecting us any way you see fit
I truly miss you, my brother, my friend
Continue to smile on us until the very end
Because we will meet again

Set Me Free: Unapologetically Me

The Playlist

When It Hurts

13. To Summer, From Cole (Audio Hug) – Summer Walker & J. Cole
14. John Redcorn – SiR
15. Seven Days (feat. George Benson) – Mary J. Blige
16. Got 'Til It's Gone (feat. Q-Tip) – Janet Jackson
17. Tyrone – Smooth Jazz All Stars

Chapter 4:
To Heal all Areas

I Choose Me

Little by little, I've been wavering away with the thought of somebody else loving me
Who needs other people's love when it keeps hurting me
I sit with the emptiness and the disparity of hurt feelings
Reliving moments where I felt nothing but heartache

I ask myself, when will you learn to let go…
Let go of people who don't understand that I am worthy
I continue to get my feelings hurt, and it seems as if I'm the only one that's forgiving
I tell myself I don't deserve this
I ask myself, do you like pain?

When I choose myself, it seems that the world is upset with me
When I tell my truth, people want to walk away from me
Change is inevitable
Knowing that the future will be different can be frightening
I look for hope and strength to keep me going
I keep my faith to help me believe
But I'm still standing to say I want better for me
I gotta choose me
The journey will be rough
But in the end… It will all be worth it
Because I will find myself

Blank Canvas

A clean new slate
The possibilities are endless
A blank canvas waits,
My dreams flashes before me in color

Starting fresh, anew,
I gently whisper, "This time, I'll get it right."
I'm trying find the light
I know my future is bright

With my eyes and heart wide open to creation's call,
I want to paint a beautiful life
A life that breaths beneath the painted scene
Where dreams and colors dance in whispered gleams

I shape my fate with steady hands,
And trusts the courage growing within me

Moments

If I could create the perfect moment
It would be raindrops coming down on a bed of flowers
Listening to the serene sounds of Mother Nature
Where it is just me connecting with the earth
Feeling the wetness of nature between my toes
And embracing what life has to offer

It's the journey of finding peace and solitude
Opening my mind to possibilities of happiness and letting it all flow in
Manifesting my goals and having creativity
Creating a safe space where there is positivity
Remembering that all things are possible through Christ

In that moment, I stop searching outward
And being to listen to myself inward
I begin to feel and let it all in
My soul is awaken
Creating spiritual awareness
It's being in the presence of the Lord
Understanding the true definition of love
Loving in truth and in action
Now that's -- true life satisfaction!

Walking with Purpose

I am no longer bounded by my hurt
I choose to be set free
I am a walking testimony
And I am somebody

I choose to be happy and heal
I choose to live
No longer will I let life pass me by
Thinking of the days when I was happy

I'm here to create new memories
I'm here to live a healthy life
With Jesus as my lord and savior
I know I can stand the test of time

Prayer and my faith has lead me to believe that I can weather the storm
It's a light at the end of the tunnel
And I am here to run towards it
This season will not last forever
But while I'm in it, I'm going to praise him

Surrender

This is my open letter to you
I been searching for something true
All this time I been looking in the wrong place
Looking for this wholeness inside of other people
And still I find nothing but emptiness

I begin to feel as if my prayer won't being answered
Until I realized I was praying for the wrong things
I come before you to be renewed
Renewed in your spirit
To be in your dwelling
To understand my true purpose in life beyond my flesh

Lord, make me over
Heal my open wounds
And create me in your imagine

I pray for a new mindset
I pray for positivity
I pray to be more open
I pray for a power of discernment
I pray to love properly
I pray and vow to be closer to you
I know now that my healing starts from within

Know Thy Self

Having knowledge is wise but knowing self is wisdom
Plant seeds for yourself so you can grow
Picture life without understanding self
What's knowledge without knowing how it can feed your soul?

Wisdom comes in phases like the moon
A constant cycle where every day is a new
From experiences and feelings
We grow to understand life and the journey that it brings
We become wise within ourselves

They say you can't teach an old dog new tricks
But every day, no matter the age, we learn new lessons
We receive new blessings

Understanding the past and present to help you know who you are today
You got to have wisdom
To make the right decisions

The Force Awakens

Made in his image
Take the time to know who you are
Could you make it on your own?
You don't need a king in order to be a Queen

You are built for greatness
But you gotta know, it comes from within
There's so much more to life
Trust me, it'll be alright

Young padawan…
Reach beyond the stars
There's many wars to be fought
But always know that the one within yourself
Is far greater than anything you can imagine

You are a student of life
With experiences and lessons
You have the knowledge to know
Self-love is the greatest power of all

Still Swimming

Time waits for no one
It constantly flows... like a stream
We continue to chase the light, we chase the dream
We fall, we rise, we lose, we learn...
And through it all, them tides still turn

As the clock keep ticking and sand falls
Life teaches us how to bend, break and still improve
Storms my come but you change, you shift... you start to see
The ocean mirrors what you could be

We have to honor time and not just hold space
When the water's cold and your vision starts dimming,
Just take a breath and keep swimming

Three decades in this thing called life,
I'm still learning through the joy and strife
Patience grows where pressure stays,
But peace arrives in unexpected ways

I'm not behind nor is it too late
So I believe that healing moves at its own rate
Healing is more than affirmations and Sunday talks
You gotta put in that work and walk that walk

Still learning
Still flowing
Baby just keep going

Healing Her

What's a soft girl era?

I like to think about it in terms of healing that little girl in me.

Young, dark, and beautiful
Full of life, so happy and bright
You have seen a lot, heard a lot, and may have felt unseen
Situations where you had no control, but you wanted to protect others
But who will protect you?

As one begins to age and mature
We realize that these things were never our fault
Feeling emptiness and living as if you were just a shadow
You are not an after thought

A soft girl era, you say?

It begins with you, loving you
Feelings confident within
Knowing that you are enough
You don't have to be so hard

Bitterness is a silent killer
So don't you self-sabotage
Let go of that hurt
And watch you elevate
To new beginnings
With a soft girl era led by GOD

Vision

Blurred in the present of hurt
Fighting the pain to understand how to let go
What is it that you fear?
Manipulation can be in the form of people pleasing and
holding on to things that no longer serve you

When the roots from the issue lies within
You have to open your mind and heart to know what it is
that you need
Finding the root to the problem seems so far fetch
But it is important to detect
What lies beneath

Peel back those layers of yourself to create that better vision
of you
Please stay true
A lot of things will break your heart, but it will fix your vision
Stay focus on inner healing
When it's internal, nothing that's external will fix it
It comes from within
Healing comes in cycles

You may think that you're learning the same lesson over and
over again
But the lesson is not over
Every new situation brings out new lessons
Don't stop your journey
Continue to shine and stand the test of time

Little Birdie

Wounded but not broken
Shaking but not weak
Flap your wings little birdie
Grow from the adversity
Self soothe the parts that hurt
Remain strong and always remember
Little Birdie in the end you will always win

Set Me Free: Unapologetically Me

The Playlist

Echoes & Endings – Letting Go

18. Since I Seen't You – Anthony Hamilton
19. I Love You – Mary J. Blige
20. Nothing To Me – Snoh Aalegra
21. Love Yourz – J. Cole
22. Another Day, Pt. 2 – Larry June
23. I Like That – Janelle Monáe

Chapter 5: Where Confidence Begins

Beauty

You are Beauty
You are Grace
Even when dripped in lace

You are illuminating as the moon
You are as exciting as the summer approaches June
You are a beautiful tune

Your skin is as pretty as nightfall
You're mixed with sweet aromas of bliss
You're a sight to see miss

You're as soothing as a winter's calm
You're as feisty as a playful lioness
You are truly royalty, your highness

I must say so myself
I am truly blessed

I am mine before I am ever anyone else's

Loving me is the only way I can truly be free
Best believe
I got me

Good Girl

Good Girl with a Hood Playlist
My confidence is at an all-time high
From my head to my toes, I feel good
The jewelry I wear compliments my skin
To me I am a perfect 10

Good Girl by nature
I am a mixture of southern cooking
With roots of Jasmine and African Royalty
Don't ever question my authority

Love potion number 9
I am aging like fine wine
Chemical X could have never made a girl this Magnificent
This right here is no experiment

Powerful indeed
I am someone that leads
I am joyfulness in the world,
As sweet, as diamond and pearls

A good girl? YES – but make no mistake
I'm fire and grace in every step that I take
Bold in spirt, strong and free
I claim my power
I am strength wrapped in fearless grace,
A queen who owns her rightful place

Noir

The color of elegance
Sophistication at its finest
It's simply chic

When you see me in all black
I'm representing power and confidence
Its dominance

I walk with my head high
I live in my own truth
Who I am has nothing to do with you
Even if I'm perceived negatively, it will not stop me
I'm a diamond in the rough
I have the spirit of a phoenix
I have a heart of a lion

I speak my mind, and that's the best way to be
I'm a black beautiful, intelligent woman
And I'm proud to be me

I walk with class and a little bit of sass
And I just might tell you to kiss my ass
A smile that will brighten up a room
And an attitude where you just might think I'm rude
I'm one of a kind

I owned my blackness
From the clothes I wear to the color of my hair
Black is beautiful

Shy Butterfly

I can see you paying attention
This is grown folks' business
And you got me reminiscing

I can see the little girl in me blushing
People think they truly know me, and they don't
My heart is low key rushing

I always been the quiet type
I remain humble and hope that you can see the true beauty of me
It's deeper than the flesh of my skin
This beauty comes from within

An introverted Social Butterfly
I don't like the spotlight
But that doesn't mean that I don't shine
To witness me is something like a delicacy

Come into my world and let's be free
Free of captivity and judgment
Share special moments with me

See this Shy Butterfly Shine
See the true beauty of me

Out of Order

She stood in the stillness of the water
Each step she took created small waves
As she calmly walked, she could see the storm
The mind was filled with broken thoughts
There was a pause behind each word that fluttered in her mind
The weight of things left unsaid grew louder

The voice within her urge for her attention
She realized she had to fix her own crown
Revisiting what makes her, her
Exploring new and old things
Would put her back in the swing

There was a quite resolve
And just like that she knew she could no longer be "out of order"

Recognizing the importance of emotional & social boundaries
The power of discernment isn't always loud
It's subtle, and you must pay attention
Things she experience no longer aligns with the peace she wanted

Even from the sign reading "Out of order"
She knew:
Right there within the stillness of the water
That some breakdowns are actually breakthroughs in disguise

Juelz

Connected like a Cuban link
Interlocked in a unique pattern that shares our stories
We're dancing in diamonds
Someone might think this the perfect story

But I see through you and the links are breaking
You can stop pump faking
You say you real
But in the end the truth prevails

When it comes to you there always lies uncertainties
Sometimes I don't know what to believe
Now I play it cool
You won't have me fool

Sneaky at its finest
You're deceiving yourself if you think for one second, you got one up
Try me, it might just be your luck
So, have your feelings on tuck
To ever think you're out smarting me
That goes against your pedigree

Your Jules do not excite me
I mean, they're pretty cheap
Your tactics are malicious
And that ain't the way I do business

Brown Sugar Queen

You're sweet aromas of earth's nature
The warmth of the sun is in your complexion
Black Beautiful Queen, you are a tropical reflection
That everyone wants to capture

Queen like Latifah, Soldier like Harriet
And a revolutionist like Betty Shabazz
When Black sons are broken, Black mothers are the cast
Beautiful Brown Woman, a black man loving you should always be task

Your love is serene
And you're worth a million dreams
You are the 5 elements of chakras
And just like the last two chakras you are light and cosmetic energy

Your colorism is baptism
Like when Jesus met Queen Sheba he was in awe of what he saw
Receiving the light and understanding the power of the divine
You will continue to shine

Don't veer away, you are the Blood Diamond they been looking for
The birth of kings who come from queens
The sunlight, the trees, and the breeze
You mean everything

She is Worth Loving

She is complex to a degree that shows she is worth loving
She is bold about her choices & views that show she is worth loving
She can be very direct & straight forward that can be intimidating, but she is worth loving
She has a smile that brightens up a room, that shows she is worth loving
She can be very sensitive where she puts a wall & become aggressive but she is worth loving
She can feed life into your soul that shows she is worth loving
She has so much love in her, once you become a part of her love line, blessing can pour out
She can be so relatable that one can find themselves feeling that they have known her for a lifetime
She has wit, style & grace
She is black & beautiful
She has charm
She is feisty & mean
She is blunt
She is authentic
She is intelligent
She can't be replace
She is not perfect, but she is very much well worth it
And that she is me....

My Girlfriends

She is the Maxine to my Khadijah
The Pam to my Gina
The Dionne to my Cher
Yeah, that's my girl

No, we're not perfect
But that's my girl, and I know she is worth it
She got my back, and I have hers
We cheer each other on to achieve the highest goals
To be our best selves

We laugh and cry together
And every moment we share is priceless
We read each other so easily
That we move as one
Oh, did I mention she a lot of fun

We are the keepers of each other's unspoken stories
Together we create the perfect category
Categories of friendship and sisterhood
What we got will always be understood

The beauty of us, is in every moment we share
The way we show up is flawless
It's called -- Love and Loyalty

So here's to my girlfriends,
The late nights,
The deep conversations,
The honesty,
To helping each other heal....

Y'all are what I defined as real

Hush Controversy

Who am I?
I am glad that you asked
I'm the backbone of every family
I gave birth to this world
Am I not important?

What would the world be without the black woman?
They try to silence us as if our voice doesn't matter
They say we are just angry
Excuse me if I'm passionate with enough love to heal a nation
The love, strength, and education to break generational curses
But you try to take our beauty and make it your own
Mask us as if we're hideous and masculine

But this Black women will persevere
I'm more than just something you can take for granted
I am human
I am soulful

Take me seriously
See that my pain is real
Speak life into me
Protect me
See that I am important
No matter what you might believe
Just know that God is in my corner

I go where I am respected
You can hate me a million times

But it will get you nowhere

Greatness is always imitated
But it could never be duplicated
I am a child of GOD
Walking with my head high and heels firm

I am a thunderstorm in silk
I wear joy like the color of my brown tone skin
My strength is wrapped in the softness of cotton
I will never be forgotten
I am rhythm and blues
Baby, I build, I bless and I bloom

The Makings of Me

Made from the strong oaks of a black man and woman
My pigment is soaked deep in melanin
The beauty of me takes precedence

You can see the confidence from my walk
The courage in me from my heart
The strength in me from my locs

From head to toe, I have a glow
My aura is made up of all the colors of the chart
You can define me as art

My vibrational frequency flows from deep within
And that's where true love begins
I am a creation of love
So I will always rise above

Strong-willed and well grounded
I will always be surrounded
By the essence of something extraordinary
Since childbirth I been legendary

I Know That I Am Greatness

I am not too much.
I am exactly enough.
Poured by God's own hands —
with fire in my bones
and softness in my soul.

I was not made to shrink
to fit beneath small minds
or disappear in rooms where I once glowed.

I am not invisible.
I just outgrew the eyes
that refused to see me.

I know that I am greatness.
I say it again.
I. Am. Greatness.
Not because the world gave me permission
but because God whispered it into me before I had a name.

My mind is divine.
My heart? A sanctuary.
My kindness? Revolutionary.

I do not need to prove
what was already written in the stars about me.

I know I'm worthy —
Of a love that listens.
A love that gives back.

A love that doesn't flinch
when I speak with depth,
when I cry out loud,
when I feel everything.

I'm not hard to love.
They just weren't brave enough to hold me.

So I turn to my words.
To my poetry.
To the place where I'm never silenced,
never overlooked,
never left on the outskirts of someone else's ego.

This is where I rise.
Where I remind myself:
Janae, you are called.
You are chosen.
You are anointed for something greater.

And no one — no one — can take that from you.

Set Me Free: Unapologetically Me

The Playlist

Soft Landings & New Beginnings

24. Brown Sugar – D'Angelo
25. Keep Looking – Sade
26. Tadow - Masego
27. Wey U (from Waiting to Exhale – Original Soundtrack) – Chantè Moore
28. Time – Sebastian Mikael
29. The Night Song – Ravyn Lenae
30. Dance Tonight – Lucy Pearl

Soundtracks to the Poetry

Set Me Free – Unapologetically Me Playlist

Nae! Make Me A Playlist!

Let this playlist hold you, even after the final word fades.
Always remember: you are not alone.
This playlist is for the parts of you that survived —
the silence,
the betrayal,
the longing.
And most of all, the rebirth.
When you begin to choose yourself,
press play.
Let the music meet you where words once couldn't.

www.ingramcontent.com/pod-product-compliance
Lightning Source LLC
Chambersburg PA
CBHW041215130526
44582CB00024BA/12